DR. FRANKENSTEIN
AND
WORLD SYSTEMS

MorningStar Publications
A DIVISION OF MORNINGSTAR FELLOWSHIP CHURCH
P.O. Box 440
Wilkesboro, NC 28697

TABLE OF CONTENTS

CHAPTER ONE

PERSONS WITHOUT BODIES

> The great enemy to the Lord Jesus Christ in the present day is the conception of practical work that has not come from the New Testament, but from *the systems of the world* in which endless energy and activities are insisted upon, but no private life with God...The central thing about the kingdom of Jesus Christ is a personal relationship to Himself, not public usefulness to men.
>
> Oswald Chambers[1]

Mary Shelley wrote a story about the disturbed Dr. Frankenstein who decided to create a human being. He steals the various parts including a head, heart, lungs, and body from a graveyard. Placing them on the operating table, he surgically fastens them all together. Then the doctor imparts life by shooting electricity into the newly assembled body and the creature awakens, slides off the table, and begins to walk and talk.

At first, as the story goes, the creature was gentle and innocent. However, because of adverse circumstances, he eventually transforms into a terror. What Dr. Frankenstein created, he could not control. The created persona took on a life of its own becoming independent, uncontrollable, and destructive.

God, as Creator, has given those created in His image tremendous creative power. This is especially evident in the conception of children. This creative power continues to function even if the man and woman do not *intend* to create, are unfit or unworthy to create, or when they do not want what they have created. This often leads to abortion or neglect. We live in a *fallen world,* therefore creative power is often misused.

Creative power is also used and misused when people give birth to a corpus or a corporation—it is a non-physical person or a *system.* In the words of Paul, this is a "person without a body" (see Ephesians 6:12 TLB). *It can take on a life of its own.* This corpus or system can be gentle and innocent or become an uncontrolled terror, doing things and creating problems never intended by those who brought it into being. Understanding this is vital. The Living Bible enables us to clearly grasp the implications of the apostle Paul's meaning in this passage:

> **Last of all I want to remind you that your strength must come from the Lord's mighty power within you.**
>
> **Put on all of God's armor so that you will be able to stand safe against all strategies and tricks of Satan.**
>
> **For we are not fighting against people made of flesh and blood, but against *persons without bodies—the evil rulers of the***

unseen world, those mighty satanic beings and great evil princes of darkness who rule this world; and against huge numbers of wicked spirits in the spirit world.

So use every piece of God's armor to resist the enemy whenever he attacks, and when it is all over, you will still be standing up. (Ephesians 6:10-13 TLB)

The nature of spiritual warfare is to knock us down and to instill despair and discouragement, but the end result is that we will **"still be standing up."** Paul seldom appeals to human willpower. It is clear that our strength is always "in the Lord."

WHAT IS A SYSTEM?

By definition a system is a group of interacting, interrelated, or interdependent elements forming a complex whole. In the courts of law we can sue the non-physical being or corporation. This corpus, as a many-membered body, is a person without a physical body. This persona has the ability to help and bless or to control and injure. It must be held responsible for its actions and the consequential results. Systems in themselves are neutral. They are vehicles that can be infused with authority and power by its participants.

In this booklet we will look at how some systems are redeemable while others are irredeemable and set for destruction or dissolution. We will also look at the kingdom as a system. If we do not actively place ourselves under the Lordship of Jesus Christ and His kingdom, then by default we are being ruled by something else. We will also see how instruction in righteousness can bring redemption to systems.

Principalities and powers operate in two realms: one in the natural world—the political, financial, and secular; the other in the spiritual—religious, church experience. I encourage readers to look up all of the biblical uses of the words *principalities* and *powers*. You will discover three things:

First, these two words are used to describe both good and evil forces—only the context determines the meaning. The tendency has always been to refer to these words as evil but this is simply not so.

Second, you will discover that some principalities are created good and then become bad. An illustration would be the creation and commissioning of a city police department. Created for a purely beneficial purpose, i.e., the protection and care of the people of that city, but if it loses its original intent and purpose, it can become infected with evil. That which was intended for good or to benefit, now becomes bad or harmful. Departing from its creator's intent, it begins to injure. With the proper leadership, instruction, and correction, it *can* be redeemed. This non-physical person can be made to do what it was created for—to protect and help the people it was supposed to serve.

Third, we discover that some non-physical persons or principalities are corrupted and are essentially irredeemable. This is first seen in the rebellion and departure of the angels. It is recorded that they left **"...their first estate..."**(Jude 1:6 KJV). The possibility of principalities being instructed and redeemed is discovered in Ephesians 3:10, **"in order that the manifold wisdom of God might now be made known through the church to the *rulers* and the *authorities* in the *heavenly places*."** God's *intent* is that created entities be instructed by the church in the ways of His kingdom and His purposes in the earth (agape love). The ones that will not or cannot be instructed must be broken or destroyed. This is seen in Colossians 2:15, **"When He had disarmed the *rulers* and *authorities*, He made a public display of them, having triumphed over them through Him."** We will come back to this again for greater clarity.

Systems are essentially neutral. They are simply a network to facilitate a certain purpose or endeavor, either good or bad. The kingdom of God is a system— the first system, which facilitates and teaches its constituents to love. Learning how the system of Christ's kingdom works, its values, purposes, and functions, is what we call "instruction (or training) in righteousness."

Paul instructed his spiritual son, Timothy, in righteousness saying, **"All Scripture is inspired by God and profitable for teaching, for reproof, for correction, for *training in righteousness*; that the man of God may be adequate, equipped for every good work" (II Timothy 3:16-17).** The Bible is the instruction handbook concerning the kingdom of God. We were not born with a natural correspondence with the ways of the kingdom of God; we were born into a fallen world system of sin. Sons and daughters of God are those choosing to be led by the Holy Spirit (see Romans 8:14) through the often costly process of gaining freedom from world systems, as well as training in how to live as a citizen of the kingdom of God.

Paul said he wanted us to be in subjection to the principalities and the powers that rule because they are governing authorities ordained by God (see Romans 13:1). To establish our theme, we read that the apostles were commanded by the principalities and powers of Rome to **"...speak no more to any man in this name" (Acts 4:17).** But they could not stop speaking what they had seen and heard, and they continued doing so (see verses 19-21). When the ruling force departs from its creator's intent, it loses or compromises its authority. We must be clear that while God gives dominion to man, He does not give away His Sovereignty.

FOUR GREEK WORDS

Far above all *principality* and *power* and *might* and *dominion*, and every name that is named, not only in this age but also in that which is to come.

And He put all things under His feet, and gave Him to be head over all things to the church,

which is His body, the fullness of Him who fills all in all (Ephesians 1:21-23 NKJV)

We need a short Greek lesson to familiarize ourselves with these four italicized words: *principality, power, might,* and *dominion.* They look like this in the original language:

Principality: (Greek: *arche*) The Greek word principality is "arche" and refers to something that has the *first* place—the *principal* ruling force or power. It is a non-physical being itself—a *thing.* Some are good; some are bad. Some can be instructed and redeemed; some are and will remain unredeemable. If a principality refuses Christ's sovereignty and His *instruction* by the church, it must be destroyed. Some are disarmed in the process of the coming of the kingdom, others are destroyed at the end. This is clearly stated in I Corinthians 15:24, **"then comes the end, when He delivers up the kingdom to the God and Father, when He has abolished all** *rule* **and all** *authority* **and** *power.*"

The word "architect" comes from the Greek word "arche." An architect is the first person to work on a project and the one with the final authority for the structure. The architect is the ruling force or the *principal* person responsible for creating the structure and to exercise final authority of what does or does not go into the building of it. He or she is responsible to fulfill the design for which the building was intended.

If an *arche* is a ruling principal, what is anarchy? It means a person or situation that has no ruling principal. Anarchy is when everyone does that which is **"...right in his own eyes"** (Judges 21:25). So, *anarchy* means there is no ruling principality and an *arche* means there is a ruling principality and that is supposed to be the Lord Jesus Christ, Creator of all principalities and powers. This is seen in Colossians 1:16: **"For by Him all things were created, both in the heavens and on earth, visible and invisible, whether thrones or dominions or rulers or authorities—all things have been created by Him and for Him."** *Arche* is also the same word used in I Corinthians 2:8, **"the wisdom which none of the** *rulers of this age* **has understood; for if they had understood it, they would not have crucified the Lord of glory."**

Power: (Greek: *exousia*). This is the authority or power by which the *thing* exercises its presence and

11

influence. The persona has either been *given* this authority or it has *assumed* it. An example is what we have *given* to the political state, a created principality, the power (exousia) to punish or put to death a violent offender. That this authority can be abused or misused is taken for granted. We live in a fallen world, administrated by sinful people.

Might: (Greek: *dunameoos*) This is the actual strength and ability to enforce the injunctions of the non-physical person. A corporation has in its by-laws the force (power) needed to implement its rule. An illustration is the Texas Ranger who is a principality or a ruling force. The badge he wears is the power/authority or exousia. The .45 caliber weapon strapped to his side is the *might*—dunamis— for the purpose of backing up his authority and instructions. Authority without the means to enforce it becomes a toothless tiger.

Dominion: (Greek: *kurioteetos*) The lordship or the sense of rulership or dominion is exhibited or exercised by the *thing.* When the *thing* is ruled and instructed by the kingdom and God's love (agape), it is a servant and seeks to establish the will and wishes of God. When it has taken on a life of its own, like Dr. Frankenstein's monster, it becomes tyrannical, oppressive, and abusive. Thus, we have Rushdooney's statement, "The state *as god* became the source of authority, morality, and dominion"[2] i.e., exercising dominion which is not legitimate. It has taken dominion other than that which was assigned. It is this illegitimate dominion that is broken at the Second Advent of our Lord Jesus. It should be stated again that though God does give dominion to man, He does not surrender His own sovereignty.

We can see all four of these words used in Colossians 1:16-20 in basically the same sequence and manner as where we have applied their meaning in Ephesians. The significance is that Paul is establishing the Person of the Lord Jesus—He is not a non-physical *Thing* but a flesh and blood Person, a real entity. He has a single will, a known mind and is capable of judgment. He is claiming and exerting His supremacy within His own realm. This is stated clearly in Colossians 1:16-20:

> **For by Him all things were created, both in the heavens and on earth, visible and invisible, whether *thrones* or *dominions* or *rulers* or *authorities*—all things have been created by Him and for Him.**

> **And He is before all things, and in Him all things hold together.**

> **He is also head of the body, the church; and He is the beginning, the first-born from the dead; so that He Himself might come to have first place in everything.**

> **For it was the Father's good pleasure for all the fulness to dwell in Him,**

> **and through Him to reconcile all things to Himself, having made peace through the blood of His cross; through Him, I say, whether things on earth or things in heaven.**

Note that the dominion of the Lord Jesus is over both **"*things* on earth"** and **"*things* in heaven" (verse 20)**. This is the kingdom of God. The Lord Jesus is a real physical Person and a literal King. His kingdom is a Principality. It is a Person, one without a physical body, yet made up of a literal many-membered body that is called the **"...one new man..." (Ephesians 2:15).**

The word "principality" is used in the Scriptures when referring to angels and demons (see Romans 8:38), but it is also used to speak about the ruling systems of the world (see Luke 12:11; 20:20). Paul shows us where principalities and powers reside: **"...seated Him at His right hand in the heavenly places, far above all *rule* and *authority* and *power* and *dominion*, and every name that is named, not only in this age, but also in the one to come" (Ephesians 1:20-21).** Jesus is seated far above all *arche* and *exousia*—principalities and powers and He has disarmed them.

In Ephesians 2:6 Paul begins to express what Christ being seated there does for us: **"and raised us up with Him, and *seated us with Him* in the heavenly places, in Christ Jesus."** If we are seated with Christ, we are seated *above all arche, authority, powers, and principalities of the world system.*

CHAPTER TWO

HOW SYSTEMS RULE

The philosopher David Hume once observed: "Nothing appears more surprising to those who consider human affairs with a philosophical eye, than the easiness with which *the many are governed by the few*."[3] Jesus wants to set us free from being governed by the few (see Colossians 2:15). Israel, by means of legalism and religious superiority, ruled the many. That rule had to be broken for the Gospel to become universal and go to the ends of the earth. Jesus insists that for us to be in His kingdom in a literal and spiritual sense, we must walk free from being governed by the few and be governed by Jesus Christ alone. Dominion of the few over the many is contrary to the intent and wishes of Father God. Entering this kind of freedom, however involves tribulations (see Acts 14:22). When the *thing* is exposed and we refuse to dance to its tune, we open ourselves to the antagonism of the system. This is one source of the tribulation referred to in the Acts passage.

SYSTEMS CANNOT LOVE

Systems cannot love, only people can love. They may profess or intend to love, but a system does not have the *capacity* to love because it is not a real person. The rationale of the system is to suppress and/or domesticate every dissenting voice. When unanimous support for the will and intention of the system is its single purpose, it has become corporate evil, the kind that has the ability to make us conform or rebel. We conform for the purpose of the pay-off—the rewards received for being domesticated. We rebel, ostensibly, for the purpose of preserving kingdom principles. Paul states it like this: **"...do not be subject again to a yoke of slavery" (Galatians 5:1).** When agape in the form of God's kingdom clashes with the ruling principality, it can be explosive. Because Christ is a real Person, He loves us and seeks to instruct us to love. This is seen in Matthew and is the pivotal concept for our understanding of the New Testament:

> **You have heard that it was said, "You shall love your neighbor, and hate your enemy."**

> **But I say to you, love your enemies, and pray for those who persecute you**

> **in order that you may be sons of your Father who is in heaven; for He causes His sun to rise on the evil and the good, and sends rain on the righteous and the unrighteous.**

> **For if you love those who love you, what reward have you? Do not even the tax-gatherers do the same?**

> **And if you greet your brothers only, what do you do more than others? Do not even the Gentiles do the same?**

Therefore you are to be perfect, as your heavenly Father is perfect (Matthew 5:43-48).

Years ago the word "profession" meant you were *called* to a particular occupation. For the most part the medical profession was born out of the agape nature of God and the church's attempt to love and care for those who were hurting and suffering. Those called to the medical field were *instructed in righteousness*, i.e., how to care. However, as we know, *systems cannot love.* Because we cannot hire people to love, the professions of medicine, law, psychology engineering, finances, etc., are quickly degenerating. The system is demanding so much for itself that it is marginalizing agape. Serving others is being turned into serving the system.

The original Christian foundations of the caring professions are being increasingly eroded and are now becoming a *system.* Think of how far the medical profession has eroded since Florence Nightingale's day. Instead of care, it has become a well-known route to wealth and prestige, and in itself is a powerful system. Patients are treated as objects, the hurting, the aged, the infirmed and the needy become marginalized and pushed to the side. The intent of the Creator is being abandoned because the focus has shifted to serving the system from serving the people.

Like the systems of Communism and Nazism, we in America are capable of rejecting those who are not usable and productive. We can do so by abortion, euthanasia, or by quietly ignoring them, relegating them to the unimportant category. It is the *system,* not people, which treat us as numbers rather than individuals, leaving us desperately wanting to be heard, loved, and understood. The *system* is what controls our behavior and diverts our love to ourselves. Systems can become self-serving and deviate from the creator's original intent.

The great leaders in the Bible were non-conformists. Individuals who, having been set free by the Person of Jesus Christ, have their security, identity, and being in God the Father. Out of this relationship they develop the capacity to love. They exhibit God's love whether they are doctors, nurses, policemen, prison wardens, military officers, clergy, or public school teachers. They can only love when they are not controlled by the system. But it is possible to be in the system and not be part of it. They love as *individuals* knowing the system itself cannot love because it is just that—a system.

CHAPTER THREE

FROM SYSTEMS TO PRINCIPALITIES

Systems may grow into ruling principalities. Picture an organ grinder at the fair with a cute little monkey on a chain. As the man rings the bell, the monkey does exactly what he was intended to do—he collects money from people who are entertained by how cute he is.

A while later we find that the monkey has grown into a chimpanzee, and beginning to resist when he does not want to do what the organ grinder wants him to. The cuteness of the money collection has dissipated, taking on aspects of *intimidation*. The chimpanzee, like Dr. Frankenstein's monster, is taking on *a life of its own*.

Finally, we picture a 600-pound gorilla standing there with the organ grinder between his teeth. When the little monkey develops into the proverbial gorilla and eats its master, good intentions and all, something has gone drastically wrong.

In Shelley's story, remember, the monster which was created could not be controlled because it had gained a life and a mind of its own. In both examples, the operative words are: *acquire, possess,* and *control*.

We create businesses, churches, and ministries like little monkeys with good intentions to serve God. Like the monkey, they are particularly good at collecting the money. The organization begins by obeying, but then one day it begins to have a strength of its own. There is nothing wrong with growth as long as it remains *instructed in righteousness*. Although growth is good, this kind of success in ministry, whether material or numerical, is not the final issue. Success is not the standard of the kingdom; it is conformity to the *will* and *wishes* of the Father alone that establishes the validity of all created enterprises. Examine the following text in this light:

> Not everyone who says to Me, "Lord, Lord," will enter the kingdom of heaven; but he who does the will of My Father who is in heaven.
>
> Many will say to Me on that day, "Lord, Lord, did we not prophesy in Your name, and in Your name cast out demons, and in Your name perform many miracles?"
>
> And then I will declare to them, "I never knew you; depart from Me, you who practice lawlessness" (Matthew 7:21-23).

JESUS AND THE SYSTEMS OF HIS DAY

Caesar and perhaps the earliest Roman senate gathered to create the Roman government of Jesus' day. It was created, slid down off the table like Dr. Frankenstein's creature, and eventually deviated from its original intent as it walked through the earth. As a *system*, Rome became formidable in conquering nations, imposing its iron rule, and domesticating the unruly. Nothing and no one could stand in its way. It was god walking the earth.

Judaism was also a ruling force in Jesus' day. It was a *system* in which the people were trapped. Although Jesus loved the Jewish people, its history and covenantal basis, He refused to conform to the distorted demands and degenerate traditions of His day (see John 5). In His challenge to these ruling systems, Jesus healed a man on the Sabbath, wreaking havoc upon the system. He was saying to the ruling principality that His Father was in authority, not them. Another Rule had come—that of the kingdom of God.

In Romans, Paul instructs us to obey the government. This sounds like a direct command until it is balanced with Peter's statement in Acts 5:29, **"...We must obey God rather than men."** Again, the question is conformity or non-conformity to the ruling system and *it is placed in tension for the purpose of balancing truth*. Dietrich Bonhoeffer, during the Hitler regime, had to chose to obey God over the government. (A most important book along these lines is *The Political Meaning of Christianity*, by Glenn Tinder.[4])

When Jesus stepped on the scene, He was completely free from the ruling systems or *arches*. He was free to love as His Father loves. Jesus loved the Romans, Pharisees, Samaritans, and the Gentiles. He had come to do away with the we/they mentality of the ruling systems. He was free to express His love to the woman at the well who had five husbands and was living with yet another man, and spoke to her about the Father (see John 4:7-23).

Jesus showed this same kind of gentleness and love toward Mary Magdalene who was a harlot. Her love for Him was so great that she did not even think about the demands and expectations of tradition or the system. When Mary anointed Jesus with expensive perfume, the Pharisee thought to himself that if Jesus were really a prophet, He would know who she was and that the *system* would not allow Him to associate with her (see Luke 7:37-39). Jesus knew who was touching Him. He also knew what motivated the response from the Pharisee. Jesus was discipling and teaching Simon how to let love (agape) rule him rather than the traditions of men and the systems of this world.

Jesus was forced to break the ruling powers of Judaism so Christianity would not become a Jewish cult. They could not and would not be instructed by the church (see Ephesians 3:10). We see that Jesus had the same response to everything, i.e., **"...I do *nothing* on My own initiative, but I speak these things as the Father taught Me" (John 8:28).** He responded exactly as the Father would respond essentially saying, "Forget your rules about the Sabbath—they are hurting people!" (see Mark 2:27-28). The principality of Judaism was seeking to exert its ruling force but Love (Jesus) was commanding obedience to the Father. Which one are we going to obey? Jesus had to separate the gospel from Judaism because Judaism had departed from its founder's intention, becoming a cruel system (see John 8:4-5). Like other persons without physical bodies, the ruling force of Judaism lurks in the shadows, repeatedly attempting to reassert its claim. The apostle Paul taught on this subject repeatedly, especially in the neglected book of Hebrews.

Think of the principalities and powers that were ruling the men and women who crucified Christ. He said, "...**Father, forgive them; for they do not know what they are doing...**" (Luke 23:34). In other words they were not familiar with the legalistic *system* and *ruling forces* that were governing their actions. They thought they were doing away with a blasphemer.

If we follow the Scriptures, it is clear that God has seen the necessity for justice in the earth by means of a sword of righteousness (see Romans 13:4). However, the very sword ordained by God can, like Dr. Frankenstein's monster, depart from its original charter. The State, embodied in the form of people like Hitler, Stalin, Pol Pot. or other tyrants, departed from their God-given mandate. We can see from these situations alone how there could be a proper time for civil disobedience in our own country.

Ordinarily when a system begins to deviate, it can be redeemed. Although I am not a historian, I sometimes wonder if this isn't why many minor revolutions have occurred, some almost without notice. Fortunately, God sent Jesus to defeat principalities and powers, and make an open show of them through the cross:

> **And when you were dead in your transgressions and the uncircumcision of your flesh, He made you alive together with Him, having forgiven us all our transgressions,**
>
> **having canceled out the certificate of debt consisting of decrees against us and which was hostile to us; and He has taken it out of the way, having nailed it to the cross.**
>
> **When He had disarmed the *rulers* and *authorities*, He made a public display of them, having triumphed over them through Him (Colossians 2:13-15).**

To understand the way principalities and powers function we can look at the life of the Lord Jesus. He illustrates it from the spiritual realm rather than the secular. The principles are the same in both realms. Paul also makes it clear that **"...we are not fighting against people made of flesh and blood, but against** *persons without bodies*—**the evil rulers of the unseen world..."** (Ephesians 6:12 TLB). Jesus, in His encounter with Peter, reveals the rulers of the unseen world without being mystical or spooky:

> **From then on Jesus began to speak plainly to his disciples about going to Jerusalem, and what would happen to him there—that he would suffer at the hands of the Jewish leaders, that he would be killed, and that three days later he would be raised to life again.**
>
> **But Peter took him aside to remonstrate with him. "Heaven forbid, sir," he said. "This is not going to happen to you!"**
>
> **Jesus turned on Peter and said, "Get away from me, you Satan! You are a dangerous trap to me. You are thinking merely from a human point of view, and not from God's"** (Matthew 16:21-23 TLB).

Jesus was not only rebuking the flesh and blood Peter for his motives, but also the spiritual force, an unseen ruler, expressing itself through Peter for the intended interruption of the purposes of God. He was **"a dangerous trap"** to Jesus. The danger was the contrary point of view, human rather than godly. Peter allowed himself to become the instrument of the *thing,* a spiritual force, at a most critical moment. I have seen this happen hundreds of times and have experienced it myself. This is not an unusual situation—it happens in everyday life: marital conflicts, church disagreements, child/parent conflicts, etc. The unseen force seeks to use our selfishness and ambition, moving us toward an end that takes from the kingdom of God and diminishes God's purpose and glory. There are cunning and *invisible* rulers and forces who serve their own evil ends by influencing essentially well-meaning men and women who think they are doing good. This is a lesson of the encounter between Jesus and Peter.

The self-referential person, when enlarged and energized by the power of the corporate system, is driven by *erithiea* (Greek), which is translated *selfish ambition*. This is the motivation of the predator or parasite. This is equally true whether these are individuals or corporations. When escalating aspirations become corporate, expressed through a system, the accumulated power overwhelms the moral intentions of the individual. Testimonies as to the corrupting power of the system in the form of Dr. Frankenstein's monster can be seen everywhere from Mai Lai to the compulsive behavior of the street gang. Think of the lessons learned in the book, *The Lord of the Flies!*

HOW A SYSTEM BECOMES A PRINCIPALITY

Over the years I have been learning to bow to the sovereign God, allowing Him to do as He pleases without saying to Him, "What doest Thou?" With that in mind, the following observations are from the perspective of my personal insight. They are not to be considered inclusive or absolute.

A system ordinarily begins as an organization created by man while some are originally created by God such as Israel and the church. It is an organization with people in it but the *system* itself is a non-physical person. For whatever reason, the entity or created organization begins to depart from its stated purpose. This can happen to any organization whether religious or secular. The further the person without a body departs from the purposes of God, the more evil, demonic, and satanic it becomes.

History shows us the departure of the church from its created purpose and the drastic measures God used to return her to the New Testament charter (see Revelation 2,3). When this departure occurs, the organization—secular or religious— no longer hears the voice of God or that of the original founders. The participants are then forced to increase effort, works, programs, or procedures to keep it alive.

Under the pressure of the emergence of the system, moral convictions and religious intent are stripped off as loose veneer. Existential pressure is so intense as to cause the philosophy to emerge that the end justifies the means. So desirous are we of self-preservation, so fearful of not being included or being rejected and suffering personal loss that even as Christians with kingdom values and convictions, we are swept up in the tide created by the ruling force. C.S. Lewis, in his small treatise entitled, *The Inner Ring,* reveals how subtle and how intense the desire to be included is. It can override and even reshape our deeply held kingdom principles.

This is a pivotal point in the life of an organization. If it was created for beneficial purposes and deviates from its created intention, it becomes a bad system. Because it has taken on a life of its own, the entity ignores, refuses, or rejects the created purpose. Invariably, its agenda begins to change, reflecting the dynamic of acquire, possess, and control. People are used and the organization, rather than its mission, becomes the central focus. The group begins to succumb to the life force the organization has taken upon itself, revealing an increased propensity toward the neglect of the hurting individual. The motive now is self-preservation of the *persona,* abusing and using the ones for whom it was designed and intended to give care. Because of the presumed *protection* of the system, individuals have an assumed anonymity and a loss of personal responsibility creating room for behavior and cruelty that would not be present if one were free from the influence of the system. Within the *thing,* we act differently than when we are apart from or on the outside of it. Every one of us have experienced this.

Once the corpus or the *thing* departs from its created intent, it becomes a ruling force. This force takes on, assumes, or is given power and authority that was not originally intended. The persona, i.e., the corporation or corpus, begins to exhibit *coercion* and *tyranny.* With some discernment, it can now be seen as a spiritual force, injuring and using people. Our attempts to avoid responsibility and employ self-justification when we see the system injure and control are enhanced by excusing negative behavior with such statements as, "Well, you can't fight city hall" or "This is just the way it is done here." The *system* not only condones wrong actions, in some cases it encourages them for the strengthening of the authority and influence of the entity. This happens not only in secular organizations but also in churches and ministries around the world.

CHAPTER FOUR

THE SYSTEM BECOMES A VIRUS

Spiritual maturity requires that we understand the nature of the non-physical person and realize the need for the *thing* to be instructed, corrected, and redeemed by the laws of the kingdom **"in order that the manifold wisdom of God might now be made known through the church to the rulers and the authorities in the heavenly places" (Ephesians 3:10).** Immediately, the problem surfaces, revealing the church—the one who should be *doing* the instructing in kingdom principles—may herself be infected with the same virus. The church, once it has lost its original kingdom charter, can give nourishment, leadership, and direction that is not only detrimental but can actually be lethal. No one can deny that individual churches and whole denominations have departed from their original charter. Once the group has departed from its king-dom *instruction in righteousness,* its nourishment is counter-productive and like radiation, is odorless and invisible. Some may remember my statement: *Mother's milk has radiation.* Receiving nourishment from the church can sometimes be deadly to the spiritual well being of those who partake, however naïve we may be.

The redeeming of a *system* is synonymous with the coming of the kingdom. It is a reassertion of the declared Lordship of Jesus Christ **"far above all rule and authority and power and dominion, and every name that is named,** *not only in this age,* **but also in the one to come" (Ephesians 1:21).** The kingdom is Christ's Lordship over all created things, governments, organizations, and ministries, down to and including our personal life. The kingdom is preceded by the word "repent" because the coming of the kingdom demands true submission (return to the Creator's original purpose) of every entity. This is seen in I Corinthians 15:24, **"then comes the end, when He delivers up the kingdom to the God and Father, when He has abolished all** *rule* **and all** *authority* **and** *power.***"** Father's creative will be **"...done on earth as it is in heaven" (Matthew 6:10)** has now been revealed to every non-physical entity. The ones capable of instruction and redemption are redeemed. Those whose total departure from the Creator's purpose has left them without value to God and His purpose are disarmed or destroyed (see Colossians 2:15). The coming of the kingdom of God suggests that in this instance and at this time, He has taken unto Himself His great power and subdues all that is contrary to the pleasure of God the Father. He is, in a loose translation, King of those kinging it and Lord of those lording it (see I Timothy 6:15). This is a unique definition of Reformation.

BECOMING DEMONIZED

We can understand lawlessness or iniquity as any created entity (physical or non-physical) that does not or will not yield itself to the Person of Jesus Christ or receive His instruction (see Ephesians 3:10). When something is not yielded to God, Satan takes advantage of the circumstances by using persons without bodies—the evil rulers of the unseen world (see Ephesians 6:12 TLB). It is important to understand that Satan does not create, he can only imitate. Evil forces can take what we have created with good intent, twisting and distorting its purpose until it can become *demonized*. This can happen in a business, local church, organization, or a school system. It can and does happen to families, to cities, and to nations. It can happen to every corpus whether secular or religious.

This may sound like an unusually hard accusation, but many church organizations miss their intended purpose, become demonized and, usually of necessity, disintegrate. When it begins to go awry, the created *thing* takes on a life of its own, slides off the table, and like the monster created by Dr. Frankenstein, changes from that which was obedient, good, and beneficial to that which is rebellious, evil, and destructive. Once it is on its way, the demonic forces invade and reinforce it. All kinds of spiritual darkness infect it. Revelation 18:2 says, **"And he cried mightily with a strong voice, saying, 'Babylon the great is fallen, is fallen, and is *become the habitation of devils*, and the hold of every foul spirit, and a cage of every unclean and hateful bird'" (KJV).** Within the category of spiritual warfare, we need to evaluate whether some systems should be disarmed or destroyed.

Paul taught us that **"our struggle is not against flesh and blood, but against the *rulers*, against the** *powers*, against the *world forces* of this darkness, against the *spiritual forces* of wickedness in the heavenly places" (Ephesians 6:12). These forces are what we are encountering and combating. I cannot emphasize strongly enough that these created things are present in both secular and religious realms. They are *world* forces and *spiritual* forces. This lesson is emphasized in the series I taught entitled, *Agape Road: Journey to Intimacy with the Father* [5]. We can fail to abide within the effective rulership of the kingdom by deviation to either one side or the other. Religious systems are in some manner more difficult to evaluate and refute because they appear and reappear clothed in the misuse of Scripture, seducing the innocent and the unsuspecting. We see this spelled out in Jesus' teaching in Matthew 23. Read the chapter again in the light of this lesson.

As a young man in the '40s, I had the dubious privilege of working for a season in the general area of the country where the infamous Hatfield and McCoy family feud occurred. You could actually feel the *ruling force* of hate and enmity in that geographical area. Some say the feud began by the inadvertent killing of one of the families' members. The ruling force was given fuel and fed by anger, hatred, and ignorance that consumed person after person. It stands now as a testimony to the reality of that which does not have a physical body, yet clearly had a life of its own, exerting a ruling force over families for many years. The end result was that Satan, the thief, came to kill and destroy.

The Hatfield/McCoy ruling force was regional. Hitler's force was global. The same principle applies to church fights. They begin with uncontrolled anger

32

and are fueled by selfish ambition that soon reveals itself as escalating aspirations. Since we may not be clearly *instructed in righteousness,* we are often unaware that we are not dealing with flesh and blood. The anger becomes energized and then demonized, leading to behavior that we would find hard to believe. These are not behaviors of the unsaved, but that which is done within the body of Christ. We can quickly slip into the mind-set of person against person rather than standing in the place of Paul's instruction that **"our struggle is not against flesh and blood"** (Ephesians 6:12).

CHAPTER FIVE

UNREDEEMABLE SYSTEMS

Principalities or systems can be either redeemable or unredeemable. The essential difference has to do with the intent and spiritual perception of its creators. The magnitude, capacity, and depth of how far we *can* depart from God and His intended purpose is described in Romans 1:18-32. God's purpose and intent is the central and definitive issue. This is true of people, organizations, ministries, and nations. Because we live in a fallen world and are born with a sinful nature, we must be *instructed* in righteousness. This is seen in Acts 17:31, **"because He has fixed a day in which He will judge the world in righteousness through a Man whom He has appointed, having furnished proof to all men by raising Him from the dead."** The corpus, the non-physical entity, must be instructed in righteousness as well. This, as we have seen, is being accomplished by the church (see Ephesians 3:10).

We know that we are not fighting against people—we are warring against a *thing* or an *it*. Nazism, created by Hitler, from its inception was a hideous evil marching through the earth gaining momentum. The clear understanding was that this force known as Nazism was indeed demonized. It was *unredeemable*. We all know that this *monster* still lurks within the German society, spilling over to other nations including our own. A force they do not understand still rules "Skinheads." This ruling force must be recognized and destroyed. It is not redeemable. However, the persons who have been captured by it are indeed the objects of Christ's love.

Communism has a similar history. In 1914, fourteen men, including Trotsky and Lenin, created a person without a body. This corpus rose and took on authority they never intended it to have. The Marx-Lenin intent was social justice to bring relief to the hurting people of the earth. Communism was *meant* to do people good and even had some biblical basis. But what was *created* was a kingdom without God.

Once it was assembled, like Dr. Frankenstein's monster, it was infused with lightning. When the stitches that held it together managed to survive, a life force was released. The creature slid down off the table and began to walk the earth. It quickly became a system or a force that ruled people with tyranny and brutal domination in nation after nation. At the time of its conception, its creators had no idea that Communism would be capable of putting two-thirds of the world under siege. It has become a monstrous principality with far-reaching implications. Militant Communism and Nazism could not be redeemed. Within the boundaries of our biblical understanding, these principalities had become demonized; consequently they rendered themselves irredeemable and had to be destroyed. It would not surprise me to see Communism return to march once again through the earth. It may do so under a different name and perhaps a different color, but it is the same non-physical persona.

Darwin created the theory of evolution. The theory soon took on a life of its own and became a principality. Now the very scientific laws it was based on are being violated in teaching evolution as fact. It is a ruling principality and even when presented with biblical and scientific evidence, it does not yield.

The Taliban faction in Afghanistan provides a vivid illustration of the power of a system. When the Taliban regime was overthrown from Kabul, the people who remained began to experience freedom from the extreme, legalistic interpretations of Islam. Beards were shaved, televisions were dug up from where they had been buried, and women, who had been forced to cover themselves from head to toe except for slits for their eyes, began casting off their prison clothes!

This demonized system of fear, hate, and abuse has been passed on to generations of their children, which eventually produced the fruit of the destruction of the World Trade Center with thousands of lives taken including their own men. Afghan children who looked to their parents for training became captives of the same system inherited by their predecessors.

The Klu Klux Klan as well as Nazism and the Taliban are examples of systems that are not redeemable for the sole reason that their initial purpose and reason for existence were wrong. There is no kingdom or beneficial purpose, irrespective of the self-deception of its founders.

We may not have grown up under such radical systems as the Taliban or Nazism, however we have all inherited or chosen the domination of one or more systems that are contrary to the kingdom of God.

REDEEMABLE SYSTEMS

The Los Angeles police force is an example of a system that had gone bad but was considered redeemable. When the Los Angeles Police Department came under federal scrutiny a few years ago, evil and corruption were identified and revealed. Attempts were made to excise the evil and corruption from the corpus.

The New York City police department is a similar example. The principality of racism, violence, and abuse of authority that ruled this police force was in the process of being over-turned. Redemption had come. The principality of the police department that had been created for a beneficial purpose was returned to that purpose, at least to a large measure.

Lifechangers, as an organization, was created in 1972. My intentions were godly and the declared purpose was to see significant teaching material translated and distributed to a minimum of twenty-five nations. Eventually it took on a life of its own. I found myself laboring long and hard to keep it alive. Expenses were paid out of my own pocket so it would continue to operate. Because I was serving it, I had to get others to serve it as well.

One day I realized it had taken on a life of its own. It had slid down off of the table and stood up, looked me square in the face and said, "I am Lifechangers, you must do what I want." When I looked at what it had become in the light of a ruling force I thought, "Lifechangers is either going to come under His kingdom and live for God or die." I stopped sending out appeals for money and minimized travel.

Then, it seemed, the very life of the Lord started to breathe upon me and the organization. We are now free from having to serve it. The system died and Lifechangers lives to serve God's purposes! This is called death and resurrection, the only route to freedom from a ruling force.

SYSTEMS OF OUR DAY

In America we have a government that is purported to be a democracy (Greek: *Demos* meaning people and *kratos* meaning power or rule). We are struggling to remain true to our founding fathers' (creators) intentions as stated in the Declaration of Independence.

> *We hold these truths to be self-evident, that all men are created equal, that they are endowed by their Creator with certain unalienable Rights, that among these are Life, Liberty and the pursuit of Happiness—That to secure these rights, Governments are instituted among Men, deriving their just powers from the consent of the governed—That whenever any Form of Government becomes destructive of these ends, it is the Right of the People to alter or to abolish it, and to institute new Government, laying its foundation on such principles and organizing its powers in such form, as to them shall seem most likely to effect their Safety and Happiness.*

America began as "one nation under God" as our Pledge of Allegiance states, but over the last fifty years has gradually but with determination, been led by factions of people away from its intended purpose and is becoming increasingly degenerate. The State has effectively departed from knowing that we were endowed by our Creator and has sought to become like God. Even when we have an election and change political leaders, replacing a Republican official with a Democrat, essentially nothing changes. Why? Because America is becoming increasingly ruled by principalities—persons without bodies, evil rulers of the unseen world. A government established by God can go bad if men give it *authority* that it was never intended to have. As it slides away from a biblical base, our need for redemption and reformation becomes more evident.

Consider a street gang as a principality or a system that exerts power and influence. Our children act differently while under their influence. I would rather face John Dillinger with his machine gun than a twelve-year-old gang member with a knife trying to reinforce his image in the gang. The child has forces ruling in his person more powerful than even he understands.

We are often astonished by the vulgar and cruel behavior that manifests itself when a rather normal individual is being carried along by the power of a mob. Think of the vigilantes of the old west. Consider how American GI's slaughtered innocent civilians in Vietnam (remember Lt. William Calley?) and the recent discoveries of similar brutality against civilians in Korea. As an individual without the ruling influence of the others, few American GI's would even consider such actions. We must understand their behavior was influenced by the ruling force, an entity, yet without a physical body. The gang, the group, the peer pressure is the ruling force which affects daily conduct.

We need to return repeatedly to the fact that it is *not* physical flesh and blood with which we are dealing. Large corporations are systems that very often become a principality which rules and dominates in an illegal, oppressive, and perhaps even a parasitic manner. The agenda for the most part is to acquire, possess, and control. If we replaced all of the top executives of any particular corporation, very little would change in the basic philosophy of the organization. All that is changed, as in our present political process, is the window-dressing and the sound-bytes.

As previously mentioned, the Democratic or Republican Party is no different. They are organizations created by men each with their own character, personality, and agenda but they are *not* flesh and blood. The results or fruit becomes the revelation of what the system is *actually* striving for. Can you imagine either party taking a full kingdom stand?

In prison there are two systems which rule—the street code (inmate system) and the system that regulates the guards and officers. There is great antagonism between the two. While conducting a regular Bible class in San Quentin State Prison outside of San Francisco, I saw how these forces ruled the inmates and these concepts became clear to me.

Systems also dominate our lives in the areas of science, technology, the media, and communications.

Television and the music world rule with tremendous power in our society, carrying our young people into realms where they should not be. This system was created by men but has absolutely taken on a life of its own, becoming a ruling force that needs to be understood and reckoned with in a biblical manner.

Several hundred years ago in England some people created a wonderful entity called the public school system. It was a system created with good intentions by human beings—free, national education for everyone. Eventually this school system climbed down off the table and took on a life of its own. In the intervening years, this created monster began to change. Progressively the people became aware that they were serving it. The principality walked through England (and on into America and many other countries) taking the children in a direction parents did not particularly want them to go. Things have not improved since.

Academia is a powerful principality. There are universities that rule entire cities. It is a force that captures and controls the professors as well as the students. It can dictate behavior, values, and dress to the point of insisting that we wear a Harris Tweed jacket, smoke a pipe, use big words, and look down our noses at anyone who is uneducated. The individual, apart from the desire to be admired and esteemed in the academic community, would seldom act this way outside of the influence of the ruling force of academia. Defeating this principality is not as easy as going to a PTA meeting and rebuking the ruling force. It is an *arche.* When someone is under a ruling force, they act differently. When you take them out from under the influence, they may once again be capable of logical thinking and biblical behavior. The good news is that Jesus rules above all principalities—everything that has ever been created. This is clear in Ephesians.

> These are in accordance with the working of the strength of His might
>
> which He brought about in Christ, when He raised Him from the dead, and seated Him at His right hand in the heavenly places,
>
> far above all rule and authority and power and dominion, and every name that is named, not only in this age, but also in the one to come.
>
> And He put all things in subjection under His feet, and gave Him as head over all things to the church,
>
> which is His body, the fulness of Him who fills all in all (Ephesians 1:19-23).

There are literally multiplied thousands of these created entities both secular and religious. Some are good, some are not so good, and some are evil. Every good system must be kept on the course of its original intent. Although the Red Cross and the Salvation Army are good systems, their leaders have undoubtedly had to struggle to preserve the creator's intent over the years.

God may not ask us to withdraw from an organization that has gone awry. He does ask us to live *in* the world but not *of* the world (see John 17:16). God may use us as part of the redeeming process of the system. Our goal, individually and corporately, is to be free from alternate ruling systems in our lives. It may cost us in many areas, however. The Lord may require you, even though you feel insignificant, to confront the whole system in love (agape) if necessary. **"And when they bring you before the synagogues and the *rulers* and the *authorities*, do not become anxious about how or what you should speak in your defense, or what you should say "** (Luke 12:11). Are you prepared for that?

CHAPTER SIX

THE CHURCH AS A SYSTEM

I have known churches that recognized that *something* was seriously and spiritually wrong in the corpus but were unable to get it redeemed. One could feel it becoming a system that could not love rather than the non-physical living body of Christ as described in the New Testament. Wise leadership will recognize that it is *not* the people but some force with a *life of its own* that has been loosed within the corporate congregation. Some of the signs are sexual confusion, division, doctrinal conflicts, and marriages/families filled with strife and control. It was and still is an *arche*, a ruling force that can be discerned as the root cause.

In biblical terms, it is a principality, a non-physical person demanding allegiance that rightfully belongs to the Lord Himself. This system is cruel and tyrannical when crossed or challenged and remains so to our day. Consider the number of people who have been injured and rejected by the church. The statistics alone tell us something is seriously wrong.

To varying degrees, this analogy is equally applicable to the many denominations of our day. If we were to wake up, we might discover our own church is a *system,* controlling our life, thinking, responses, and planning. It has taken on a life force of its own, one that we never imagined or intended. We may find ourselves defending, protecting, and funding this entity in ways that are analogous to Dr. Frankenstein and his monster. Some faithful pastors and churchgoers should consider this in light of past or present church fights and other internal struggles that have been neither understood nor resolved. Please understand what I am saying is an observation and not accusation.

When Jesus was hanging on the cross He knew it was the system, not the two soldiers who crucified Him. Jesus asked the Father's forgiveness for the two soldiers because they did not know what they were doing (see Luke 23:34). Political Rome, itself a system, was energized and provoked to this act of crucifixion by degenerate Judaism which became a system. Remember it is not "flesh and blood" that we are dealing with, although these non-physical beings are almost always run by a small executive group or a single person with nearly unlimited authority. They must create the illusion that it is a larger entity so that they can have the power to acquire, possess, and control. Almost without exception, it produces tyranny.

Because we are dealing with fallen man, it is inevitable that the *arche,* once it has taken on a life of its own, leads to the fulfillment of personal agendas as well as unbridled selfishness and ambition. *Escalating aspirations become the ruling force.* Think of the self-serving African rulers, or the Marcos of the Philippines who were recently exposed and deposed. This same principle can be seen repeatedly in the church and in the apostolic company who

"...all seek after their own interests..." (Philippians 2:21). What could we possibly expect in the rest of society? Someone once said, "For as the church goes, so goes society!"

When a system degenerates to the place where it can only acquire, possess, or control, the system becomes unavoidably *utilitarian*: it *uses* people as cannon fodder. We can be used by the world, and the church can also use us. There is essentially little or no difference except one does so by using Bible verses.

Johnny Cash sang a western song about a mining company that says: "I owe my soul to the company store." The lyrics were basically, work a week, borrow from the company store, and go deeper in debt. The "company store" is a clear expression of how we allow systems to rule our lives. The system now *owned* him. Freedom was gone; the cycle was in place. The company was invested with *authority* and everyone was in awe and fear. The company had *power*—useful, practical, punishment to all who complained—those who resisted did suffer. Finally, the company had *dominion*—it exercised its lordship in the place of the Lord Jesus and His kingdom, creating the injustice of which the Bible speaks.

What is frightening to me is that I have known, been part of, and led Christian churches which functioned exactly like this company store. This is why we are taught to pray daily, effectively, and fervently that **"Thy kingdom come Thy will be done, on earth!..."** (Matthew 6:10).

Tradition itself can become a ruling force. It is a system that says, "We have a certain way of doing things that cannot be disturbed." Tradition tends to cultivate a false sense of importance, belonging, and identity. It also tends to insulate us from getting involved with anyone outside our particular group. Although country club settings have the reputation of holding fast to tradition, churches are also steeped in it. It doesn't even seem to bother us that as a church we are not doing what Jesus instructed—to care for the prisoner, widows, orphans, and the poor.

The apostle Peter struggled with tradition. He saw the kingdom and was commissioned to leadership by Christ. However, when the Judaizers arrived from Jerusalem, Peter caved in to their pressure of tradition. Even though Peter's faith knew better, the *thing* had arrived from Jerusalem, the pressure of which influenced and changed his conduct, causing Peter to refuse to be associated with Jesus and then with the Gentiles (see Galatians 2:12). Think of it! If it can happen to Peter who walked with Jesus, it can certainly happen to us.

Many of us have responded to tradition in a similar manner. It is a kind of pressure, a ruling force, the power and strength of which is enormous. Only the person who has a clear sense of the kingdom, one who has security, identity, and belonging in Christ can resist the sheer strength of the ruling force when it exerts its influence upon us. This allows us to understand the necessity of placing our love and affection on the person of our Lord Jesus Christ. It is only our love for Him that is strong enough to resist the pressures to conform (see Romans 12:2).

Is the kingdom of God a principality? Yes. Jesus Christ should be the principle force that rules our life. Jesus was certainly ruled by a Principality—His Name is God the Father, a non-corporeal Being who exerts His will and influence in all the earth. This kingdom of God has a King who walked the earth as the Son of God and Son of man. He is a physical being who looks a lot like us for the purpose of bringing us individually and corporately under His Lordship of Jesus Christ. God's government does not work on the principles of acquire, possess, and control but according to God's own nature which is agape—wooing, and appealing us to give ourselves to Him for the unfolding of His eternal purpose in our lives. We need to remember that when an earthly kingdom shakes, the kingdom of God does not shake.

As a people of destiny, we must discern what is ruling us. Not what we *say* is ruling us, but what is actually ruling us. Psalm 139:1 says, **"O Lord, Thou hast searched me and known me."** The thought of that can really scare some of us, especially if we suspect some force other than God rules us. Sometimes anointed ministries can react in unpredictable and violent ways when you touch the principality this rules. Jesus lifted us above all principalities and we are supposed to be able to look down at all of them, understanding that they have, indeed, been disarmed.

Just because something is born of God does *not* mean it cannot depart from its original intent, resulting in negative effects (see I Corinthians 11:17, 22). It grieves me to watch the call to ministry increasingly become a *system*. Our love should never bow to success; we must learn to bow only to the will and wishes of God as our Father.

Is Jesus our Lord the ruling force in our lives or is it some *thing* of which we may not even be fully conscious? If we are ruled by a system, then we begin to promote the system and not the kingdom.

Over the years, God has sent His Spirit to us for revival and reformation. Slowly, but effectively, we turn the visitation into a man-made creation. When the life of God is no longer the impetus, it begins *to take on a life of its own,* becoming a system. After it becomes a system, people wonder what happened to the "good old days" of the movement. This could serve as a brief history of denominationalism. Missionaries go to foreign countries to establish the kingdom of God. However, if they are locked into a system, they establish their denomination rather than the kingdom of God. Eventually good intentions and human love run out because systems cannot love—only the fresh anointing of the Holy Spirit enables us to love. The people in these foreign countries wonder what we are exporting from America when they see denominational distinctions rather than the love of Christ and unity. We need to remember that this problem is not a person of flesh and blood but a zeal that is not according to righteousness (see Romans 10:2).

Recently, a pastor friend of mine described how he literally lost his position as pastor at a small fundamentalist church because he broke tradition by cooking soup for some hungry migrant workers from Mexico. The church was offended because he "contaminated" their special cooking pot. Chances are this same church was sending money and missionaries to Mexico! We would like to think that we are more mature than this, but we are not. If we do not identify the strength that these systems carry, we cannot understand the kingdom and do what is necessary to allow the love of God to break their ruling power over us.

Many churches have, without knowing it, become a system. John Knox, who founded the Presbyterian denomination, never had any intention of it becoming what it has become today. Presbyterianism, having swept the earth, stood up having taken on a life of its own, demanding to be served. Likewise, Martin Luther, whose goal was to *reform* the Catholic Church, pleaded with everyone not to start a new denomination in his name. God asks us to keep the systems we create pure and open to His ways but most of the time we think *we know* what is best.

DISCIPLESHIP AS A PRINCIPALITY

In the 1970s and 1980s there was a move of God called "Discipleship." Its intent was godly: the restoration of integrity to pastoral care and personal accountability in the Charismatic renewal. It was born of God and was under His direction for a number of years. Many needs were met and marvelous things were happening in the areas of belonging and cultivating mature Christian character. The goal was not someone to make decisions *for* us but that we should not have to make them alone. There was a sense of community and healthy relationships holding us accountable to God and to one another.

However, according to the very principles we are describing, discipleship became a system that hurt people. Because it became a system, it could not love. To our great pain and sorrow, wrong and injurious *extremes* soon overshadowed the biblical principles that were being taught. Many of us as leaders did not lead as servants in love (agape) which resulted in the unhealthy and unbiblical submission of men. Many people who embraced this movement found it easier to relinquish their responsibility of walking in faith with God, choosing instead to blindly follow their pastor. If circumstances did not unfold to their satisfaction, the pastor was the one to be blamed. Discipleship sat up on the table demonstrating it had a life of its own. It slid down off the table, and like Dr. Frankenstein's monster, turned into something very ugly. It walked the earth as a ruling force that pillaged and plundered. Its power was underestimated. Alone and out from under the influence of the ruling force, each of us were normal people. When we place ourselves under a ruling force we partake of its life, philosophy, and influence, and our behavior responds accordingly. **"Do not be deceived: 'Bad company corrupts good morals'"** (I Corinthians 15:33).

Seeing these biblical principles distorted was the greatest pain of my life. My understanding of how systems take on a life of their own is partially a result of that journey. It took me a long time to make the public apology given to the body of Christ in 1987 for two reasons. First, I believed deeply in the principles we were teaching. Second, I did not realize how far the movement had deviated in practice from its original purpose and teaching. I was not aware of the full extent of the departure and misuse until years later.

We can mistakenly think that because God births something, He cannot or will not kill it. If we are sensitive to the working of the Holy Spirit, we will not continue on with something that should die. God is a jealous God (see Exodus 34:14). He does not allow His purposes and wishes to be subordinated to anything in the lives of those who belong to Him. There are no convenient formulas; He asks us to follow Him in faith.

TAKEN CAPTIVE

Colossians 2:8 says, **"See to it that no one takes you captive..."** Can we be a Christian and a captive at the same time? Absolutely. This is what we identify as a spiritual POW—prisoner of war. There are men and women in ministry, attempting to help others, who are captives themselves. II Peter 2:19 is very clear about **"promising them freedom while they themselves are slaves of corruption; for by what a man is overcome, by this he is enslaved."**

Our danger is to *think new* and *act old*. If we do not actively place ourselves under the Lordship of Jesus Christ, then by default we find ourselves being ruled by something or someone else. Jesus said it this way, **"Nor do men put new wine into old wineskins; otherwise the wineskins burst, and the wine pours out, and the wineskins are ruined; but they put new wine into fresh wineskins, and both are preserved" (Matthew 9:17).** Can you see the old wineskin as a principality?

There can be several ruling forces other than the Person of the Lord Jesus dominating our earthly existence. These forces can exert their influences at the same time, creating a turmoil and confusion that seems unexplainable, if not mysterious. Certain systems and principalities are so much an integral part of our lives that we may not even realize what is happening.

Obviously, we are not physically taken captive—it happens in our mind, and takes hold of our will and then is revealed in our conduct. II Corinthians 10:5 says, **"We are destroying speculations and every *lofty thing* raised up against the knowledge of God, and we are taking every thought captive**

to the obedience of Christ." These lofty things have been part of our culture, beliefs, attitudes, and values for a long time and some, frighteningly enough, may have even been taught to us by our families. This is another example of mother's milk having radiation. Not only are *we* taken captive and ruled by these various systems or principalities, but we may *insist* that our loved ones come under it also. There are certain families that rule like dynasties. Not only can a family become a principal ruling factor, they have authority and power to injure us and do things to make us uncomfortable if we do not capitulate to their rule. This is what lays behind Jesus' statement about loving Him more than our earthly mother and father. It is a matter of breaking the *rule* of things that control us other than the Person of Christ.

Think for a moment of how we behave—positive or negative—when, as full-grown adults, we visit our parents' house. In our desire to please them we do things and say things we would never do in our own home. When someone comes under the influence of a principality, his or her behavior changes. Sometimes, if we were alert, we can actually watch and experience our own behavioral change when we come under the influence of the ruling force. Once we are out from under the principality or ruling system, we behave differently.

We need to develop a greater sensitivity to what it is like to live under the freedom of the government of the kingdom and the Lordship of Christ as compared to a world system or perhaps a religious one. The intent is His kingdom being first in the life of His followers resulting in our freedom.

CHAPTER SEVEN

CASTING DOWN PRINCIPALITIES

When we discover ourselves serving the *system*, even captured by that which we may have created, we must know how to get free. The *arche* or the ruling power, as we have learned, is a *persona*, an entity without a physical body, an evil ruler of the unseen world (see Ephesians 6:12 TLB). In the larger body of Christ there is the belief that you can simply "take authority and cast down the principalities." We must understand how this works in practicality because the Bible teaches us that we *can* discern their presence, assess and expose the ruling forces and powers which have degenerated and departed from their created intent.

It must be clear that once the power of an *arche* is discerned and broken, that the whole system then has to be *instructed* as to the intent of God's original purpose (see Ephesians 3:10). The parallel is similar to casting out a demon from an individual. The person, while delivered from the power of the demonic force, has yet to be *instructed in righteousness,* lest continued ignorance allows the demon to return with seven others! It is also possible that this *thing*, this non-physical entity, may be essentially irredeemable and may need to be dissolved or broken for the long-term purposes of God and His kingdom. This is called the Father's sentence of death. Some forces simply need to be disarmed—their power, authority, and dominion destroyed or taken away. Colossians 2:15 says, **"When He had *disarmed* the rulers and authorities, He made a public display of them, having triumphed over them through Him."**

Allow me to create a hypothetical illustration. A kingdom-oriented pastor, sincere and determined, takes the responsibility to lead a particular church. It could be any church in any town of any denomination. Quite rapidly he discovers this church body he now pastors has seriously departed from the created purpose of the founders. What no one understands is that they are being ruled by a force or principality. To complicate matters, this force seems to give them what they want, demands little from them, and is deeply rooted in tradition and the town's culture.

The mission statement—their constitution and by-laws—clearly describes what the congregation was intended to accomplish. If he managed to break the spiritual principalities and powers that hold this congregation in its grip, he then would have to *instruct them in righteousness* (see Ephesians 3:10). Can you imagine what his job description would look like and what kind of leadership, suffering, and struggle he and his family would have to embrace? The pastor may feel that the changes needed are too difficult and are simply not worth the effort. After all, there are greener pastures. So he leaves and another "innocent" pastor comes, causing the cycle to repeat ad infinitum. The congregation thinks all the problems are the pastors' fault. The pastor thinks it is the peoples' fault. Both have been deceived and as a result are confirmed in their error. The kingdom goes lacking due to their ignorance. That church, which was supposed to be the Father's House—the center for the government of the kingdom of God on the earth—continues as a religious club whose candlestick has been removed. Now we can understand Jesus' words concerning the whitewashed tombs, which on the outside are beautiful, but on the inside are full of dead men's bones (see Matthew 23:27).

Paul uses these words "casting down principalities" repeatedly to help us understand the kingdom, power, and supremacy of Christ. He sees our grasping this truth as fundamental, a necessary part of knowing God, understanding His love, and walking in His kingdom. Consider the well-known Romans passage in this light:

> But in all these things we overwhelmingly conquer through Him who loved us.
>
> For I am convinced that neither death, nor life, nor angels, nor *principalities*, nor things present, nor things to come, nor *powers*,
>
> nor height, nor depth, *nor any other created thing*, shall be able to separate us from the love of God, which is in Christ Jesus our Lord" (Romans 8:37-39).

If the system detects for a moment that you are not loyal to its ruling force and somehow you are perceived as refusing to buy the package, you will be persecuted. You could lose your promotion, your retirement, other benefits, or even your job for not conforming. You can lose your membership and may not even know why you were dismissed. The excuses and accusations are often "rebel" or perhaps "Jezebel." The truth is you have become a threat to the ruling system. Do not be intimidated by all of the corporate or religious incantations. Take yourself outside of the camp where Jesus is and identify with Him (see Hebrews 13:13). Walking free from the *arches* that will cost you. "**Through many tribulations we must enter the kingdom of God**" (Acts 14:22).

WHY WE NEED REFORMATION

In Romans 13, Paul tells us to obey the government as a principality ordained of God. This precipitates the much discussed question of whether to conform or not conform to the laws of the land. Because the kingdom of God is revolutionary, its nature presents us with the problem of civil disobedience. Do we obey God or man? In Romans 13, Paul is seeking to modify that revolutionary tendency, seeking to avoid human reactions which are motivated by selfish ambition and are always counter-productive.

Francis Schaeffer predicted that there would be conflict between the constraints of the kingdom of God and world systems in his small but important book entitled *A Christian Manifesto*[6]. No one, in my opinion, could have written such a straight and needed insight into how ruling forces function in our own society. Schaeffer said the day was fast approaching when the principalities ruling our nation will have departed so far from God that Christians would be forced to choose God and His kingdom over the laws of the land. This was written twenty years ago.

There will come a time in Western society when we may have to resist and refuse our own government. As long as it is in any way doing what it is supposed to do, we are commanded to obey it and respond properly because it is the ruling force and as such is ordained by God. The opposite, we must remember is anarchy, which is most troubling with every man doing that which is right in his own eyes.

My wife and I recently watched for the third or fourth time Schaeffer's video series from the 1970s entitled, *How Shall We Then Live?*[7] We can see the issues of the systems of our society more clearly today than when Francis Schaeffer first gave us these insights. Our nation was originally founded on biblical standards of love and liberty. My prayer is that God would give us a gully washing reformation, not just a revival, which would turn this and other nations toward Himself.

Years ago God brought reformation to Great Britain through John Wesley. That reformation dealt with slavery, changed the child labor laws, closed the bar rooms, addressed the issues of financial injustice, and shook up the entire country—a revival that brought real and lasting change rather than just emotional response. Reformation does not mean legalism or more rules, but a revelation of His government and Lordship. It means that we are learning to bring our organizations as well as ourselves under the Lordship of Jesus Christ. Reformation, properly understood, means the breaking of the *arches* and ruling forces, wherever they may be.

FATHER'S SENTENCE OF DEATH

What must happen to a system so that it can be redeemed and reformed is called the Father's sentence of death. I have seen this happen to many systems that have had their beginning in the purposes of God. According to our example of discipleship, it had to be disarmed because it was not capable of or open to being *instructed in righteousness*. God promised to shake everything that can be shaken, **"...the removing of those things which can be shaken, as of *created things*, in order that those things which cannot be shaken may remain"** and so that **"we may offer to God an acceptable service with reverence" (Hebrews 12:27-28).** His kingdom is the only enduring authority. He gives man dominion; He never surrenders His own Sovereignty. God wants us at all times and in all situations to allow agape to be the one ruling force in our lives.

There are different types of death that happen to a system or organization. The following are four that a missionary friend shared with me:

1. *Natural death*: When something lives its full cycle of life and then dies, i.e., plants, animals, humans, buildings, etc.

2. *Warfare*: When war, persecution, satanic inter-vention, or aggression causes people's lives to be cut short.

3. *Inevitable and consequential judgment*: When God cuts a life short because of sin. Some examples are King Herod, Ananias and Saphira, etc.

4. *The Father's sentence of death*: This corresponds with the Father's will and command before the full cycle of life is complete. That which has been born of God, anointed and protected is now sentenced to death. God has His own reasons and purpose for doing so—illustrated in the

premature death of Jesus Christ at thirty-three years of age.

Allow me to repeat myself. We are mistaken when we think that once something is born of God, it should live forever! When anything or anyone begins to take on a life of its own, *apart from the intent of its creator,* it has the potential of becoming a monster and begins to rule us instead of our being able to direct it toward the intended purpose. We end up serving it rather than it serving God. The longer it goes without the Father's sentence of death, the more it begins to degenerate. This is the time when it comes closest to becoming demonized. Decay begins to set in rather than metamorphosis. Nothing is changing and death is everywhere.

Our pet projects and beloved systems that have received a death sentence from God the Father are like the cowboy in an old Western movie. Although fatally shot he refuses to fall down and die. He staggers all over town demanding attention, bleeding, and traumatizing everyone before he gives up.

Just because God birthed a ministry does not mean it should live forever. Even when something is born of God, has been anointed, and has hope for the future, God may ask us to trust Him through the death sentence. If we refuse to hear Him, the ministry, business, or organization begins to degenerate. When we are not sensitive to the Holy Spirit, we administer spiritual CPR, adrenalin shots, and electro therapy to keep the heart beating. Continued resuscitation does not mean we are within the borders of His will. We need to learn the difference between resurrection and decomposition. If we continue in this course of action, there may still be people who are helped, but there can be others who are hindered or hurt in their walk with the Lord.

Look at the life of the apostle Paul. He was establishing churches everywhere he went until one day the Father said it was time for him to be shut up in prison. I am sure the Father's sentence of death on Paul's ministry was a painful experience. However, apart from his time in prison, we would not have been given the Prison Epistles.

The Lord may ask us to be confined in some way. When we embrace it by letting go of our program, His rejuvenating life and love flows through us. We may say, "But, Lord, that would kill me." He says, "Now, you are getting the message!" This is kissing the cross.

THE PROBLEM WITH CONTROL

The following are ten suggestions why those of us who struggle with the problems of acquire, possess, and control may be *unable* to hear the Father's sentence of death:

1. *The golden calf of our system*. The church, our ministry, calling, title, or position in an organization or office has become what we worship in place of God Himself. We believe this, like the golden calf, is what brought us out of Egypt. We dare not give up our chance for bigger, better, and higher rewards in an organization that was initially created for His purposes. All of this is defended as "God's will."

2. *Fear of the unknown*. Death is the ultimate trust in the Person of God. Death of anything leads to a period of de-centering and uncertainty. The

sense is that any form of death must be avoided because death is an enemy.

3. *Preservation of reputation.* We are striving to find our own identity as contrasted to who we are in Christ. Paul states that Christ made Himself of no reputation. Part of the death and resurrection is the surrender of our reputation, secular or religious, into the death process.

4. *Preservation of the comfort level and being undisturbed.* Death changes everything and everyone. We do not know what will be expected or demanded of us on the other side of death and resurrection. We choose to keep what we know, because we are unsure of what things may look like after resurrection. The change may be too much to embrace and not worth the risk.

5. *Loss of control.* Death is the ultimate loss of control. Only God is in charge of resurrection. The need to stay in control is the root of the tradition that rules nations, cities, churches, and families.

6. *Fear of people's opinions and ideas.* The voices of friends and enemies are a strong motivational factor in all decisions. Fear of man is a snare (see Proverbs 29:25). We preserve the status quo because of our refusal to embrace the misunderstanding that may come from family or the rest of the evangelical world. This is a clear sign of a ruling force other than that of the Person of the Lord Jesus Christ.

7. *Fear of failure.* Life has so many failures. Failure, especially in the realm of the spiritual is unbearable. We are ruled by the fear of failure because we cannot risk another one.

8. *Confusion and uncertainty in the voice.* Is this really the Father's death sentence or do we just need to pray harder, read extra Scripture, and fast more? Could God really be asking us to let this die?

9. *Fear of repeating painful lessons of the past.* Having once been successful and knowing what loss is, we decide that success is preferable. Success now holds us in its grip and we will do anything to avoid a painful experience. The whole idea of death is not a popular theme in the charismatic or evangelical world.

10. *Bargaining.* This is trying to make a deal with God rather than embrace the cross. That which is self-referential within us does not die easily. Striking bargains can be seen in the lives of many Bible characters. I will do this, *if* You will do that. As a Father, God understands and deals with us accordingly. However, surrendering is always less expensive than bargaining.

God is relational but because many of us carry a secret fear of Him, we do not make ourselves completely available to Him. He is our only source of security, identity, and belonging. Many times when ministering to others we feel adequate, loved, and rewarded by them. We are taking the "well-done" from the wrong source. In God's presence, however, we don't experience that same sense of adequacy, freedom, or comfort level. Because of this we give ourselves to ministry and not to Him. This, I am certain, is one of the meanings behind the text we examined in Matthew 7:23, **"depart from Me, you who practice lawlessness."**

Abraham, the father of our faith, was severely tested when God asked him to offer his son as a burnt offering. He struggled with what God was asking him to do, but eventually he acquiesced, picked up the knife, and yielded to God's perplexing command. God said, "**...now I know that you fear God, since you have not withheld your son, your only son, from Me**" (Genesis 22:12).

There are five things about Isaac that were similar to Jesus. They were both: 1) promised by God and born of God; 2) anointed sons; 3) the hope of the future; 4) protected and beloved; and 5) an instrument of blessing to others.

God spared Abraham's son, but did not withhold His only Son from us. He loved us with such a great love that He allowed Jesus to be betrayed and then sacrificed on our behalf. Jesus was tested and grieved to the point of death (see Matthew 26:37-39). Jesus wrestled with His Father but always yielded to Him. It is possible that Jesus would like to have stayed on the earth for a few more years to accomplish more good.

God in His own mysterious way uses death to defeat death. When He knows we are serious about surrendering to Him alone, resurrection results in victory, cleansing, and supernatural power.

The Father's sentence of death is the path for blessing and resurrection life. When the Father's sentence of death is spoken over some aspect of our lives, remember He may only require that the knife be raised over our head before He stops it. In other situations, He requires actual, literal death. If we are determined to obey His voice concerning something

He birthed through us, He may give it back to us in resurrected form. If and when He does, it is no longer a system but a force which has been redeemed by the instruction of the church as seen in Ephesians 3:10.

AGAPE AS THE RULING FORCE

Jesus asked, **"and why do you call Me 'Lord, Lord', and do not do what I say?" (Luke 6:46).** It is because the principality or system that we have chosen, or by which we have been captured, prefers to serve the needs of our self-referential agenda. When we are not walking in pure love for God and openly surrendering to Him, we are serving some other *thing.* We do so for the return or pay-off, gaining some *reward* that is illegal and illegitimate. Jesus addressed this when He said not to do things to be noticed by men (see Matthew 6:1). These are illegal pay-offs that are neither of God nor of His kingdom.

We can prevent the person without a body from taking control by keeping a kingdom agenda. As we focus on the Father, we can bring the system or person without a body back into alignment without killing it. In an effort to come out from under the power of a system, we may find ourselves fighting people, but remember **"our struggle is not against flesh and blood..." (Ephesians 6:12).** When we focus on submitting to Jesus as Lord, He is faithful to break the dominating force and lead us to freedom. If we try to love when the *system* is ruling us, we eventually run out of good intentions and human effort. He will make us free enough to love as He loves. To be "perfect" (see Matthew 5:48) means to be mature in our ability to love as the Father loves.

As the church we are called to **"bring to light what is the administration of the mystery which for ages has been hidden in God, who created all things; in order that the manifold wisdom of God might now be made known through the church to the *rulers* and the *authorities* in the heavenly places" (Ephesians 3:9-10).** The mystery, which has now come to light, is the Gospel message. Challenging a principality must be done in plurality and in the Lord's timing.

In John 17:23 Jesus prayed to His Father, **"I in them, and Thou in Me, that they may be perfected in unity, *that the world may know* that Thou didst send Me, and didst love them, even as Thou didst love Me."** This is the communal reunion of creation. It is the chosen end of the New Testament revelation, as seen in John 17:21-26. We are challenged to learn to love God above *all* else and He will enable us to love people everywhere without hidden agendas. We do not have to *trust* them to love them. When the world sees this kind of love and unity, they will know who He is. This is the prophetic hope of all of God's people.

May our Lord Jesus teach us how to love people, all the while recognizing the *oppressive* principalities that function behind the scenes in the lives of others as well as our own. We are called to be "seated with Him in heavenly places far above all *rule* and *authority* and *power* and *dominion* and every name that is named" (see Ephesians 1:18-23). It is from this position alone that we can love as the Father teaches us to love (see Matthew 5:48).

Now flee from youthful lusts, and pursue righteousness, faith, love and

peace, with those who *call on the Lord from a pure heart*.

But refuse foolish and ignorant speculations, knowing that they produce quarrels.

And the Lord's bond servant must not be quarrelsome, but be kind to all, able to teach, patient when wronged,

with gentleness correcting those who are in opposition, if perhaps God may grant them repentance leading to the knowledge of the truth,

and they may come to their senses and escape from the snare of the devil, having been held *captive* by him to do his will. (II Timothy 2:22-26).

SUMMARY

We have learned that there are good systems and bad ones. If you find yourself part of a system that has deviated from its original intent, it may be redeemable. In light of this, consider the following seven principles that we have discussed:

1. Know that "...the truth shall make you free" (John 8:32).

2. Learn how to be trained in righteousness (see II Timothy 3:16).

3. Know that our security, identity, and belonging are in Christ (see I Corinthians 3:23).

4. Know that we have the authority and responsibility to cast down principalities (see Romans 8:37-39).

5. Understand our need for reformation (see Romans 13).

6. Embrace the process of the Father's sentence of death if necessary (see Romans 8:12-13).

7. Allow agape to be the ruling force (see John 17:23).

PRAYER

Father, we freely acknowledge You and Your Son as the Lord of lords. Your Name is above every name and we yield ultimate obedience to You alone. Help us to identify the principalities and powers, the ruling forces, which unceasingly seek to dominate and control. Reveal to us the areas in which we are selling ourselves short by yielding to systems that prevail in our own culture.

We choose to take Your yoke upon us. We want to be free to love as You love. We recognize that there are hurting people in every nation waiting to know about Your love. Cause us to communicate with You and with others in reality and truth. Let our actions be truthful. Enable us to take the kingdom, the Person of Christ, and the love of God to others without being wrongly influenced by a ruling force or controlled by a system. Father God, set us free so that we can love as You love! In Jesus' Name, Amen.

ENDNOTES

[1] Chambers, Oswald *My Utmost For His Highest,* October 19. Oswald Chambers Publications Association, Barbour and Company, Inc., Uhrichsville, OH, 1935, 1963.

[2] Rushdoony, R.J. *Institutes of Biblical Law,* Craig Press, Westwood, NJ, 1973 .

[3] Hume, David as quoted by Joseph Sobran in The Washington Times, October 16-22, 2000.

[4] Tinder, Glenn. *The Political Meaning of Christianity: An Interpretation,* Louisiana State University Press, 1989.

[5] Mumford, Bob, *The Agape Road: Journey to Intimacy with the Father,* Lifechangers, Raleigh, NC, 2000.

[6] Schaeffer, Francis *A Christian Manifesto*. Crossway Books, 1981.

[7] Schaeffer, Francis, *How Shall We Then Live?* Gospel Films, Muskegon, MI, 1981.